Spanish Decorative Ironwork

with over 300 Illustrations

edited by
Luis Labarta

DOVER PUBLICATIONS, INC.
Mineola, New York

Copyright

Note copyright © 2000 by Dover Publications, Inc.
All rights reserved under Pan American and International Copyright Conventions.

Bibliographical Note

This Dover edition, first published in 2000, is a selection of 120 illustrations from Volumes I and II of the work *Hierros Artisticos*, originally published c. 1901 in Spanish and French by Francisco Seix, Barcelona. The introductory Note and captions have been specially prepared for this edition.

DOVER *Pictorial Archive* SERIES

This book belongs to the Dover Pictorial Archive Series. You may use the designs and illustrations for graphics and crafts applications, free and without special permission, provided that you include no more than ten in the same publication or project. (For permission for additional use, please write to Permissions Department, Dover Publications, Inc. 31 East 2nd Street, Mineola, N.Y. 11501.)

However, republication or reproduction of any illustration by any other graphic service, whether it be in a book or in any other design resource, is strictly prohibited.

Library of Congress Cataloging-in-Publication Data

Hierros artísticos. English. Selections.
    Spanish decorative ironwork : with over 300 illustrations / edited by Luis Labarta.
        p. cm. — (Dover pictorial archive series)
    Selections from Hierros artísticos, originally published: Barcelona, Spain : F. Seix, 1901.
    ISBN 0-486-40962-7 (pbk.)
    1. Ironwork—Spain. I. Labarta, Luis. II. Title. III. Series.
NK8262 .H54213 2000
739.4'746—dc21

00-027559

Manufactured in the United States of America
Dover Publications, Inc., 31 East 2nd Street, Mineola, N.Y. 11501

Publisher's Note

The following illustrations from *Hierros Artisticos* (or *Artistic Ironwork*), originally published in Barcelona circa 1901, is a representative sampling of some of the finest examples of Spanish decorative ironwork from the tenth to the eighteenth centuries, with a special focus on pieces created by the masters of Castile and Catalonia. In fact, many of the cathedral grilles included in this volume may still be seen today in and around Barcelona, as well as in other great Spanish cathedrals. Toward the end of the book are a smaller number of plates containing examples of decorative ironwork from other western European countries—particularly France, Germany, and Italy—spanning much the same time frame as the Spanish pieces.

Prior to the fifteenth century, Spanish ironwork was essentially similar to that being produced in France and England, except for the so-called "Mudéjar" style. This distinctive blending of Gothic with Moorish elements was the product of the many gifted Moorish craftsmen who were enticed to remain in Spain while most of their brethren were pushed further south. It was not until the Renaissance period (circa 1450–1525), however, that Spanish decorative ironwork reached its zenith, particularly during the sixteenth century, in the form of the monumental cathedral grilles mentioned above. These *rejas*, as they were known in Spanish, reached twenty-five or thirty feet in height, and their function was to separate the high altar of the cathedral from the nave; a second *reja* became necessary when the choir was moved from the transept. Ironsmiths were eager to avail themselves of the opportunity these *rejas* presented for the practice of their art, amply demonstrating their extraordinary skill and power over the solid and unyielding iron. In many of the large cathedrals in Spain, two of these immense *rejas* are found facing one another.

The present volume also includes numerous examples of Spanish ironwork on a smaller scale: in gates, balconies, door and window grilles, lighting fixtures, brackets, locks and keys, door-knockers, wrought-iron pulpits, domestic objects, and the like. It was the custom of the time as well to decorate doors with elaborate nailheads or embossed studs, as may be seen from several of the illustrations on these pages.

As for the ironwork of other countries of western Europe, it is notable that French mastery in the art didn't blossom until the accession of Louis XIII to the throne in 1610. This monarch, a worker at the forge himself, inspired a new movement in the field of ironworking which spread to adjoining countries, investing its practitioners with new energy and momentum. No longer was the art of a simple character, but instead became more versatile and imaginative, eventually leading to the introduction of the rococo style in 1723, which was also imitated by the craftsmen of the adjacent countries.

During the Renaissance in Germany, ironsmiths were their own designers, often conceiving of intricate plans to show off their considerable skills. Ironwork was found everywhere and for every purpose: in churches, window grilles, gates, door-knockers, handles, hinges, keys, escutcheons, locks, sign brackets, etc. Nonetheless, the peak of German achievement in the art was ushered in by the baroque and rococo periods, when iron smiths attained an unparalleled perfection of detail and skill. Wrought iron was manipulated as if it were a plastic material, extravagantly molded to the whim and will of the craftsmen's conceptions.

CONTENTS

(page numbers and captions numbers are one and the same)

Ironwork of Spanish Origin

1. Andirons, fireback, and a small fork, Spanish (Castilian), 14th and 17th centuries
2. Andirons, Spanish (Catalan), 14th and 15th centuries
3. Brackets, German and Spanish (Catalan), 17th century
4. Brackets, Spanish (Catalan), 15th, 16th, and 17th centuries
5. Brackets, Spanish (Catalan), 17th century
6. Church brazier, scales, and embossed studs, Spanish (Catalan), 14th, 15th, and 17th centuries
7. Candelabra and chandeliers, Spanish (Catalan), 13th and 14th centuries
8. Candelabra and finial from a grille or cupola, Spanish (Catalan), 13th and 17th centuries
9. Candelabra or torch-stands, Spanish (Castilian), 17th century
10. Candelabra, Spanish (Catalan), 11th, 12th, and 13th centuries
11. Candelabra, Spanish (Catalan), 12th and 14th centuries
12. Candelabra, Spanish (Catalan), 13th century
13. Candelabra, Spanish (Catalan), 14th and 15th centuries
14. Candelabra, Spanish (Catalan), 15th century
15. Pulpit, Spanish (Castilian), 16th century
16. Pulpit, Spanish (Castilian), 16th century
17. Pulpit, Spanish (Castilian), 17th century
18. Chandelier, Spanish (Catalan), 14th century
19. Chandelier, Spanish (Catalan), c. 14th–15th century
20. Chandeliers, Spanish (Castilian and Catalan), 16th century
21. Funeral chapel, Spanish (Catalan), 14th century
22. Chest, Spanish (Castilian), 15th century
23. Tombstone cross and candelabra, French and Spanish (Catalan), 17th century
24. Processional cross and lectern, Spanish (Catalan), 16th and 17th centuries
25. Boundary crosses and embossed stud, Spanish (Catalan), 16th and 17th centuries
26. Grille and boundary crosses, Spanish (Catalan), 15th and 16th centuries
27. Domestic objects, Spanish (Castilian), 17th century
28. Domestic objects, Spanish (Castilian), 17th century
29. Cathedral door-knocker, Spanish (Catalan), 14th century
30. Gothic door-knocker, Spanish (Catalan), 15th century
31. Door-knocker, Spanish (Catalan), 16th century

32. Door-knockers and door-pulls, Spanish (Catalan), 14th and 17th centuries
33. Door-knockers, French and Spanish (Catalan), 13th and 15th centuries
34. Door-knockers, Spanish (Castilian and Catalan), 16th century
35. Door-knockers, Spanish (Catalan), 15th and 16th centuries
36. Door-knockers, Spanish (Catalan), 15th and 16th centuries
37. Door-knockers, Spanish (Catalan), 16th and 17th centuries
38. Door-knockers, Spanish (Catalan), 16th century
39. Door-knockers, Spanish (Catalan), 17th century
40. Abbey door, Spanish (Catalan), 10th, 11th, and 12th centuries
41. Roman door, Spanish (Catalan), c. 10th–13th century
42. Small alcove door, Spanish (Catalan), 16th century
43. Embossed door studs, Spanish (Castilian), no date
44. Door, Spanish (Catalan), 12th century
45. Gridirons, Spanish, Flemish, and French, 17th century
46. Cathedral grille, Spanish (Castilian), 16th century
47. Cathedral grille, Spanish (Castilian), 16th century
48. Cathedral grille, Spanish (Castilian), 16th century
49. Cathedral grille, Spanish (Castilian), 16th century
50. Cathedral grille, Spanish (Castilian), 16th century
51. Cathedral grille, Spanish (Catalan), 15th and 16th centuries
52. Cathedral grille, Spanish (Catalan), 15th century
53. Cathedral grille, Spanish (Catalan), 15th century
54. Cathedral grille, Spanish (Catalan), 15th century
55. Cathedral grille, Spanish (Catalan), 16th century
56. Chapel grille, Spanish (Castilian), 16th century
57. Church grille, Spanish (Catalan), 16th century
58. Hospital pharmacy grille, Spanish (Catalan), 17th century
59. Palace door grille, Spanish, 18th century
60. Palace grille, Spanish (Castilian), 16th century
61. Palace grille, Spanish, 18th century
62. University library grille, Spanish (Castilian), 16th century
63. Grille and balcony railing, French and Spanish (Catalan), 16th and 18th centuries
64. Grille fragment, Spanish (Catalan), 11th or 12th century
65. Grille, Spanish (Castilian), 15th century
66. Grille, Spanish (Castilian), 16th century
67. Grille, Spanish (Castilian), 16th century
68. Grille, Spanish (Catalan), 13th, or beginning of 14th century
69. Grille, Spanish (Catalan), 15th century
70. Window grille, German and Spanish (Castilian), 15th and 16th centuries
71. Details of various grilles and embossed studs, Spanish (Catalan), 15th and 16th centuries

72. Top portions of two grilles, Spanish (Catalan), 16th century
73. Handles, pulls, and furniture hinges, German, French, and Spanish (Catalan), 15th century
74. Keys and locks, French and Spanish, 15th and 17th centuries
75. Keys, Spanish (Catalan), 14th, 15th, and 16th centuries
76. Keys, Spanish (Catalan), 17th century
77. Keys, Spanish (Catalan), 18th century
78. Embossed nailheads or studs, Spanish (Castilian), 15th, 16th, and 17th centuries
79. Pull-rings, door-knocker plate, and drawer-pull, German and Spanish, 15th and 16th centuries
80. Balcony railing, Spanish (Catalan), 18th century
81. Balcony railings, Spanish (Catalan), 18th century
82. Scissors, Spanish, 17th and 18th centuries
83. Washstand and Weathervane, Italian and Spanish (Catalan), 15th century
84. Weathervane, Spanish (Catalan), 18th century
85. Framework of a well, Spanish (Catalan), 15th century

Ironwork from Other Western European Countries

86. Andirons, French and Italian, 16th century
87. Andirons, French, 13th, 15th, and 16th centuries
88. Brackets and candelabra, French and Italian, 16th, 17th, and 18th centuries
89. Brackets and grille, French and German, 15th, 16th, and 18th centuries
90. Brackets, French, 18th century
91. Tripod brazier, tripod, Italian, 17th century
92. Chandelier, French or Italian, 15th century
93. Chandeliers, French, 17th century
94. Door-handles, German, 15th century
95. Door-knocker plate and escutcheon (keyhole plate), German, 15th and 16th centuries
96. Door-knockers or pull-rings, German, 15th and 16th centuries
97. Door-knockers, Swiss and Italian, 15th and 17th centuries
98. Door hinges, French and German, 12th, 14th, and 17th centuries
99. Door, German, 15th century
100. Door, tabernacle, German, 14th century
101. Escutcheons (keyhole plates), German, 16th, 17th, and 18th centuries
102. Chapel grille, Italian, 17th century
103. Door grille, French, 18th century
104. Church grille, French, 12th century
105. Section of a chapel grille, Italian, 16th century
106. Cathedral grille, German, 15th century
107. Grille, French, 17th century
108. Grille, French, 17th century
109. Grille, French, 17th century

110. Grille, French, 18th century
111. Grille, French, 18th century
112. Grille, German, 15th century
113. Grille, German, 15th century
114. Grilles from a carriage entrance, German, 16th century
115. Furniture hinges, escutcheons (keyhole plates), and embossed stud, German, 15th century
116. Keys and locks, French and German, 15th and 17th centuries
117. Lock, key, and furniture bolt, French, 13th and 14th centuries
118. Pull-ring, lock, and embossed corner studs, German, 15th century
119. Staircase and balcony railings, French, 18th century
120. Sign or emblem bracket and hinge, German, 15th and 16th centuries

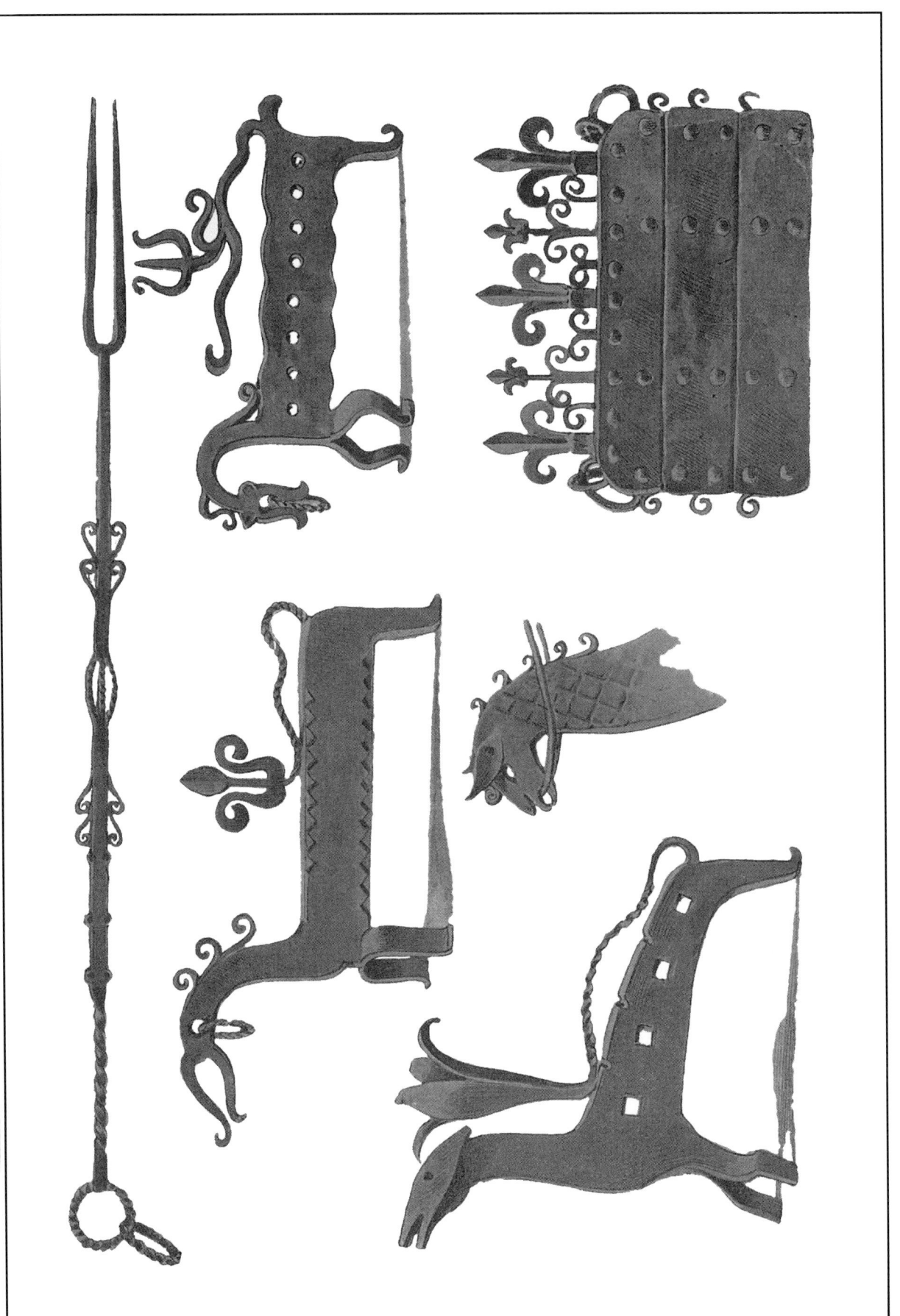

1. Andirons, fireback, and a small fork, Spanish (Castilian), 14th and 17th centuries

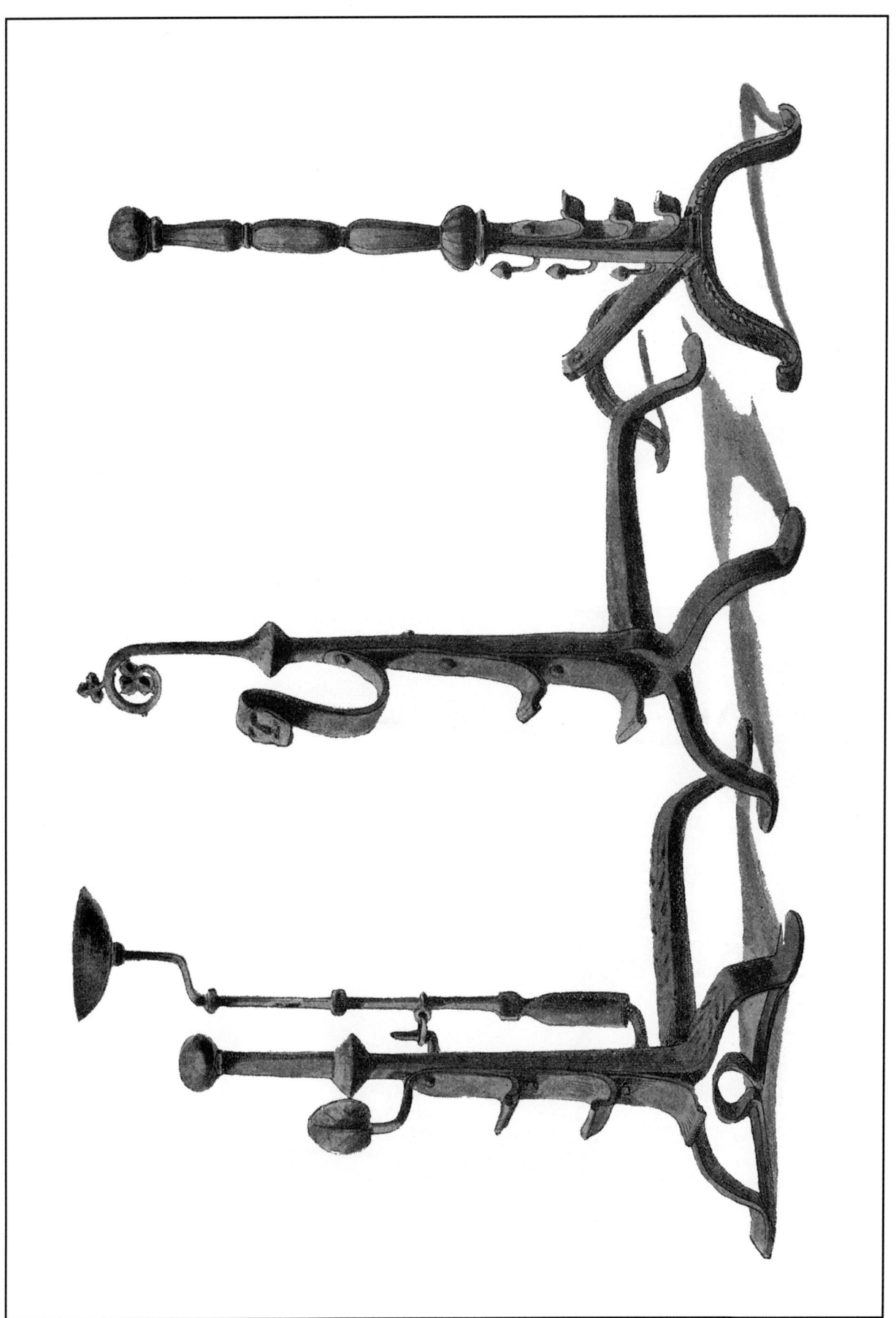

2. Andirons, Spanish (Catalan), 14th and 15th centuries

3. Brackets, German and Spanish (Catalan), 17th century

4. Brackets, Spanish (Catalan), 15th, 16th, and 17th centuries

5. Brackets, Spanish (Catalan), 17th century

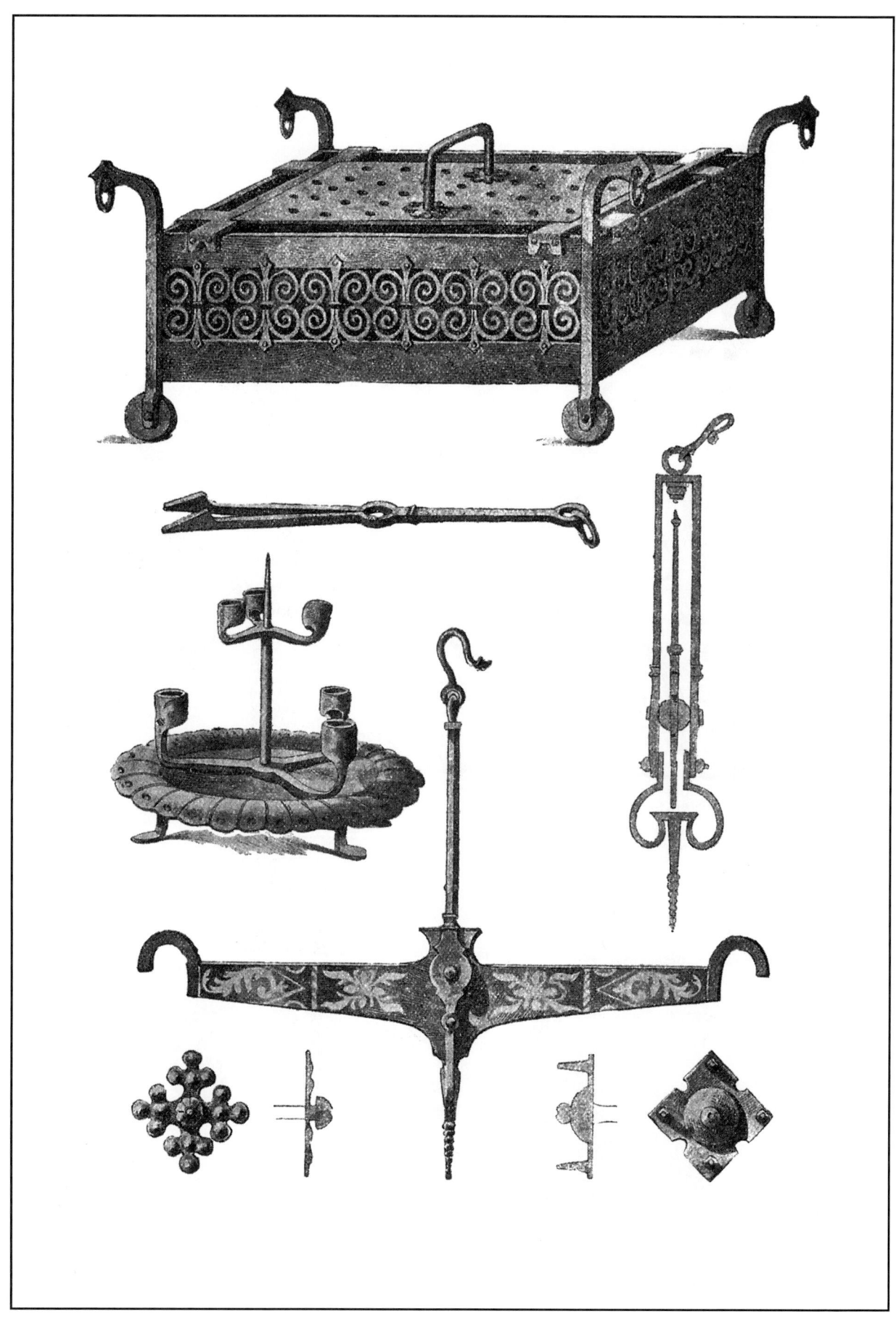

6. Church brazier, scales, and embossed studs, Spanish (Catalan), 14th, 15th, and 17th centuries

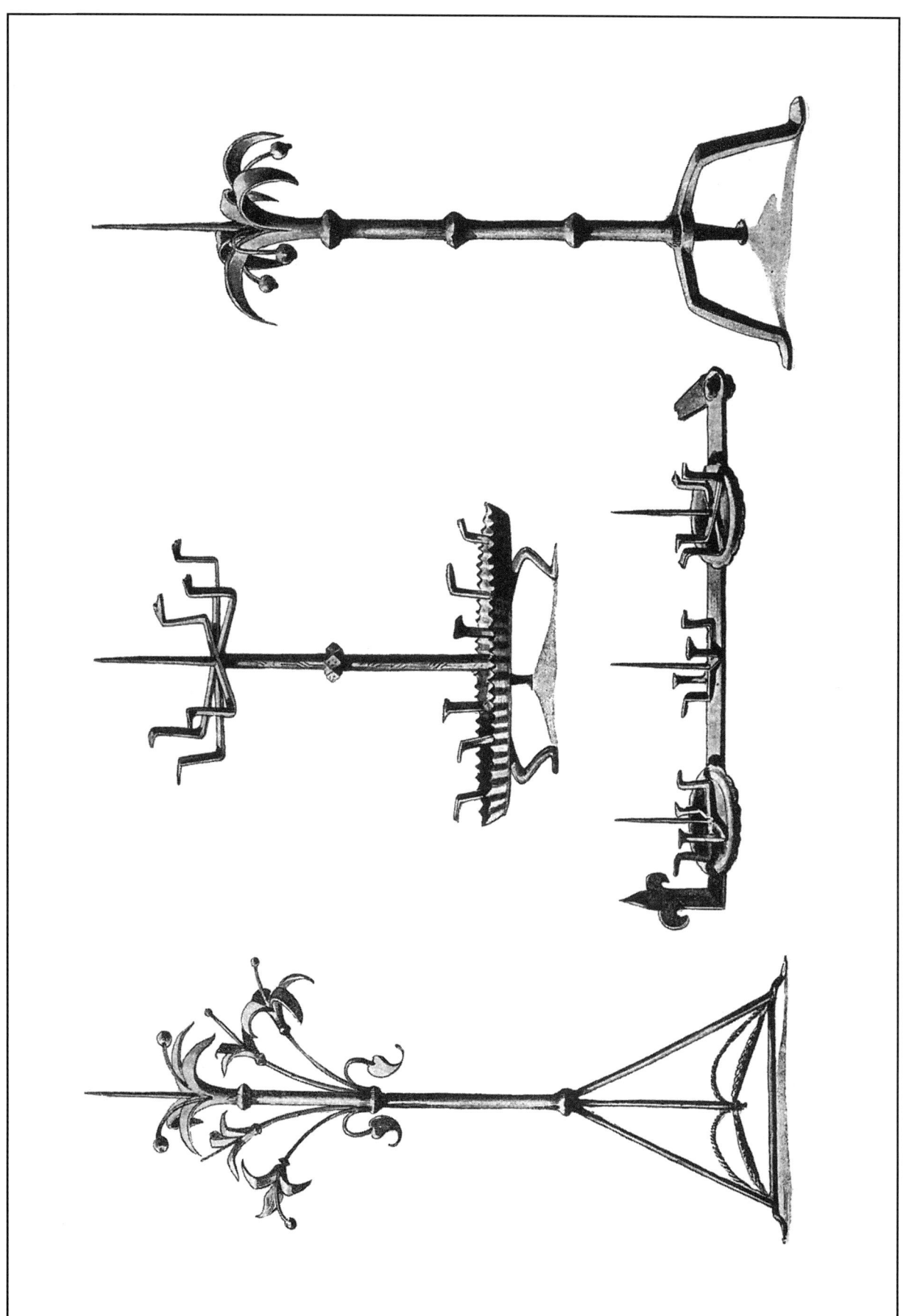

7. Candelabra and chandeliers, Spanish (Catalan), 13th and 14th centuries

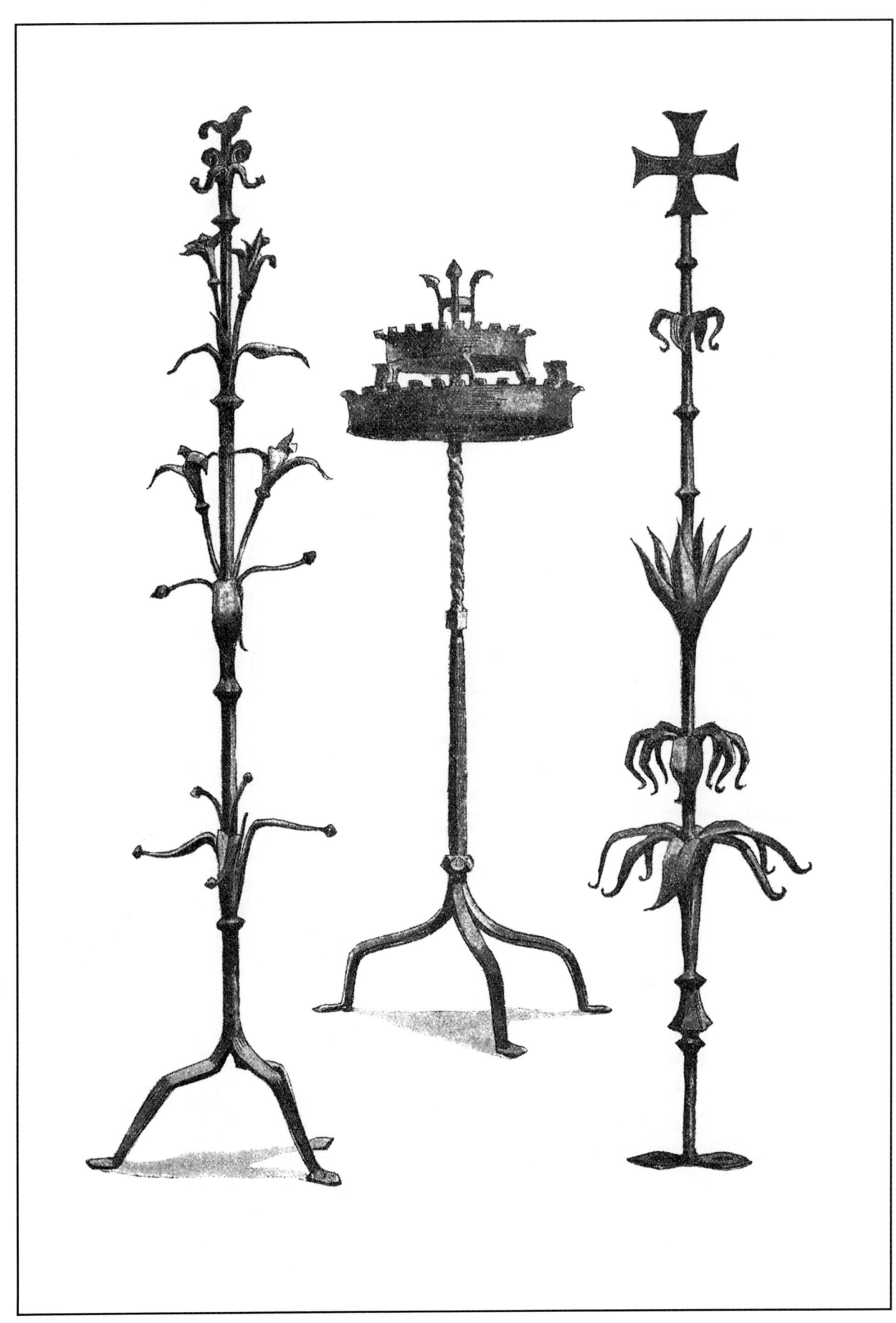

8. Candelabra and finial from a grille or cupola, Spanish (Catalan), 13th and 17th centuries

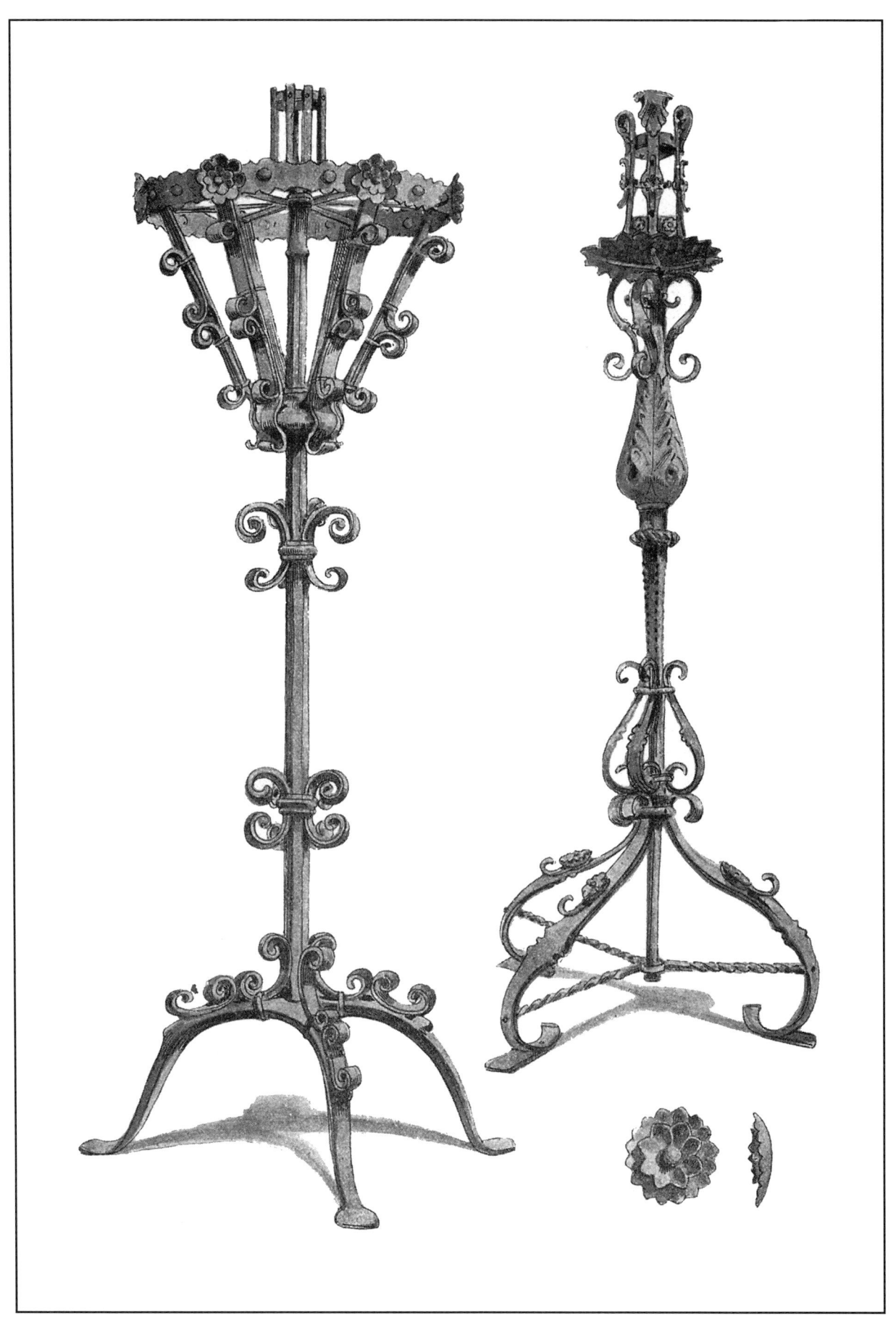

9. Candelabra or torch-stands, Spanish (Castilian), 17th century

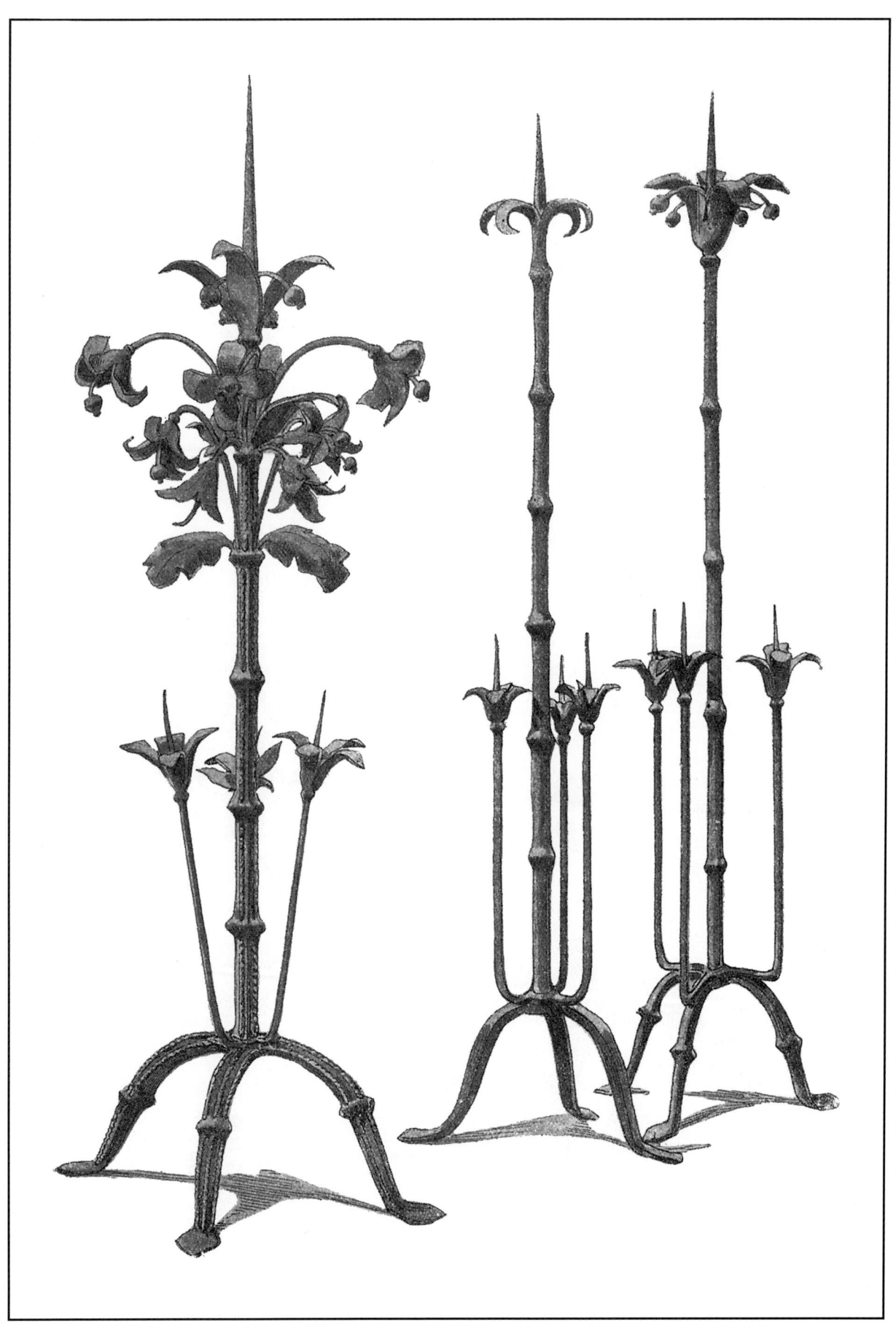

10. Candelabra, Spanish (Catalan), 11th, 12th, and 13th centuries

11. Candelabra, Spanish (Catalan), 12th and 14th centuries

12. Candelabra, Spanish (Catalan), 13th century

13. Candelabra, Spanish (Catalan), 14th and 15th centuries

14. Candelabra, Spanish (Catalan), 15th century

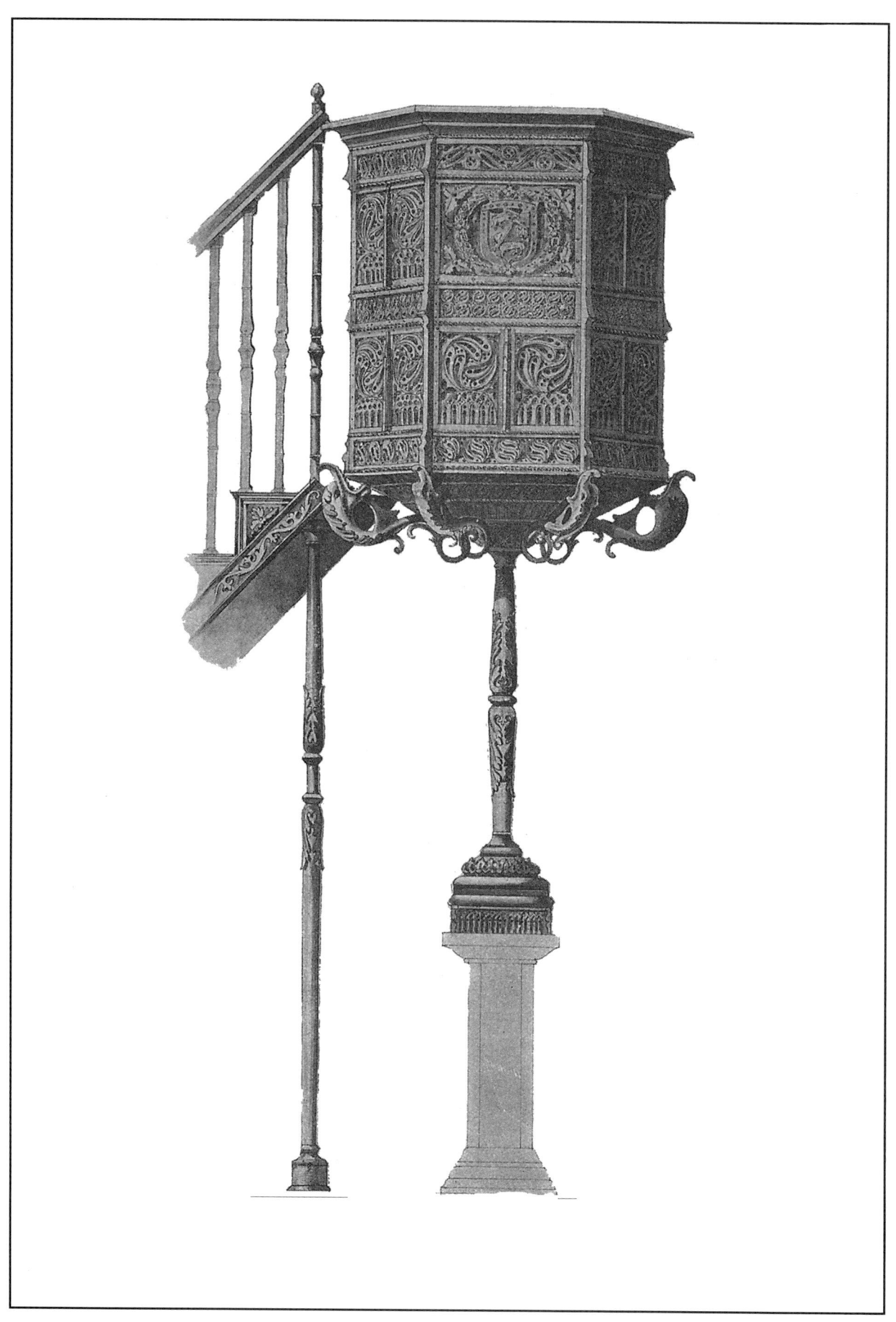

15. Pulpit, Spanish (Castilian), 16th century

16. Pulpit, Spanish (Castilian), 16th century

17. Pulpit, Spanish (Castilian), 17th century

18. Chandelier, Spanish (Catalan), 14th century

19. Chandelier, Spanish (Catalan), c. 14th–15th century

20. Chandeliers, Spanish (Castilian and Catalan), 16th century

21. Funeral chapel, Spanish (Catalan), 14th century

22. Chest, Spanish (Castilian), 15th century

23. Tombstone cross and candelabra, French and Spanish (Catalan), 17th century

24. Processional cross and lectern, Spanish (Catalan), 16th and 17th centuries

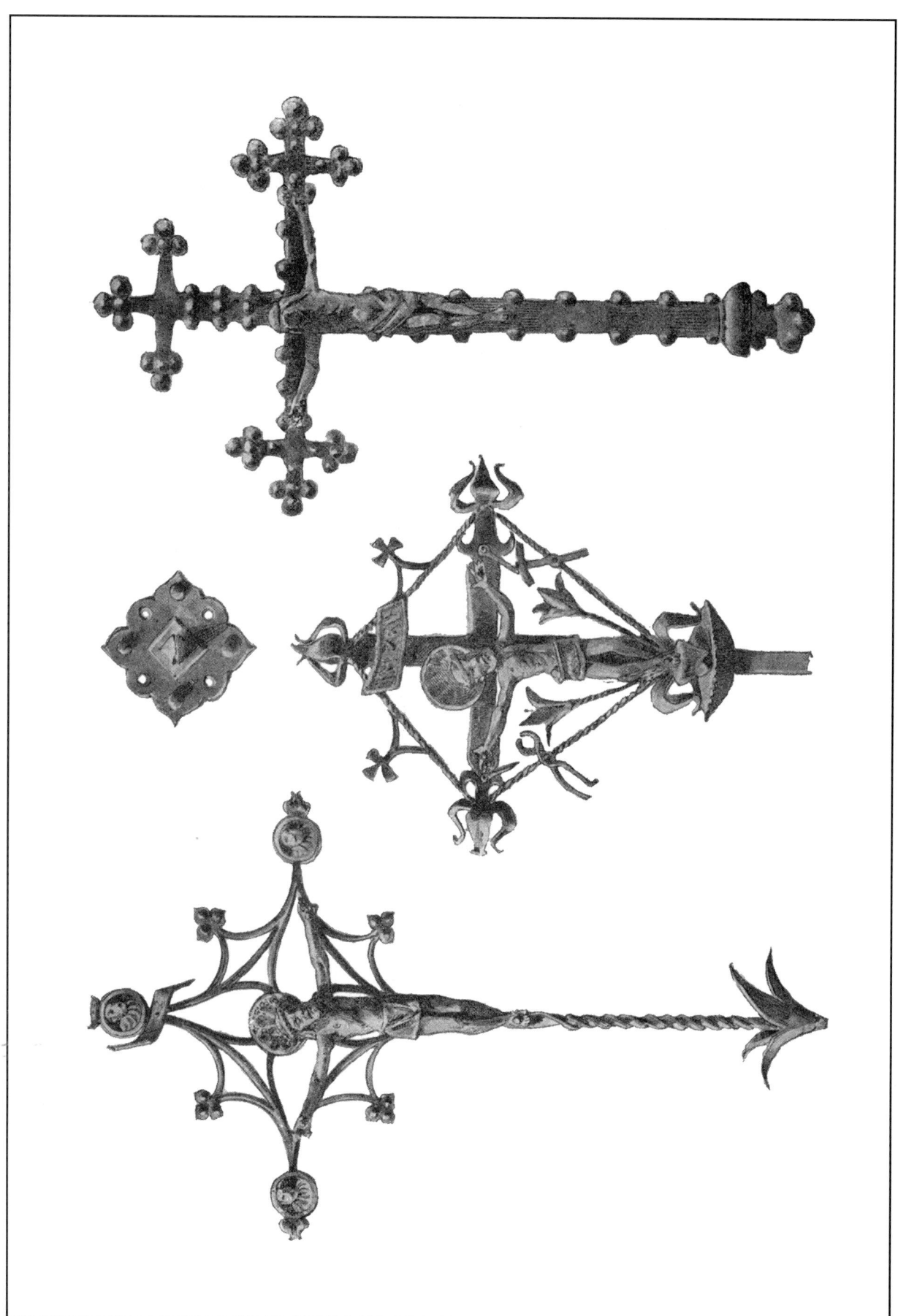

25. Boundary crosses and embossed stud, Spanish (Catalan), 16th and 17th centuries

26. Grille and boundary crosses, Spanish (Catalan), 15th and 16th centuries

27. Domestic objects, Spanish (Castilian), 17th century

28. Domestic objects, Spanish (Castilian), 17th century

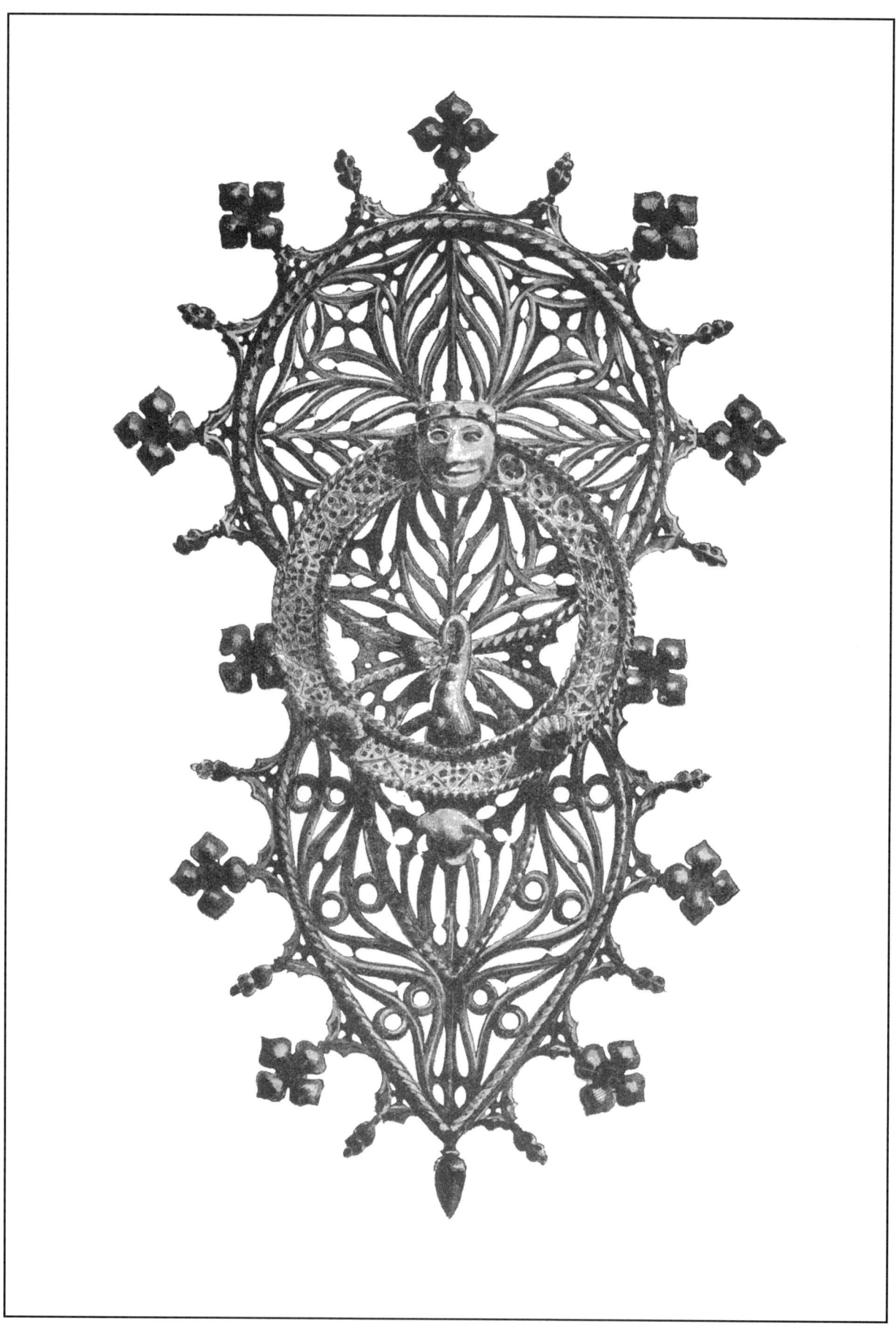

29. Cathedral door-knocker, Spanish (Catalan), 14th century

30. Gothic door-knocker, Spanish (Catalan), 15th century

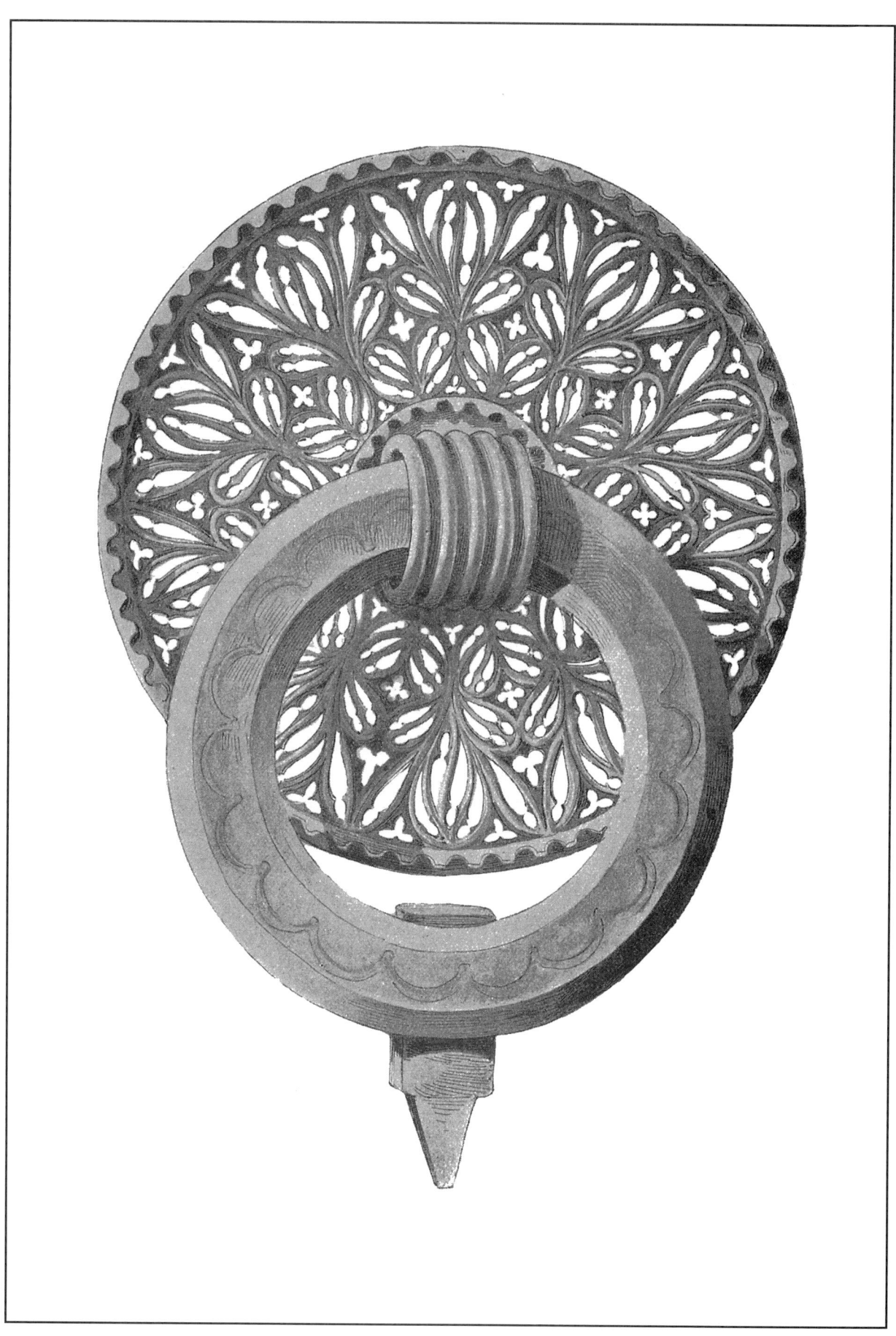

31. Door-knocker, Spanish (Catalan), 16th century

32. Door-knockers and door-pulls, Spanish (Catalan), 14th and 17th centuries

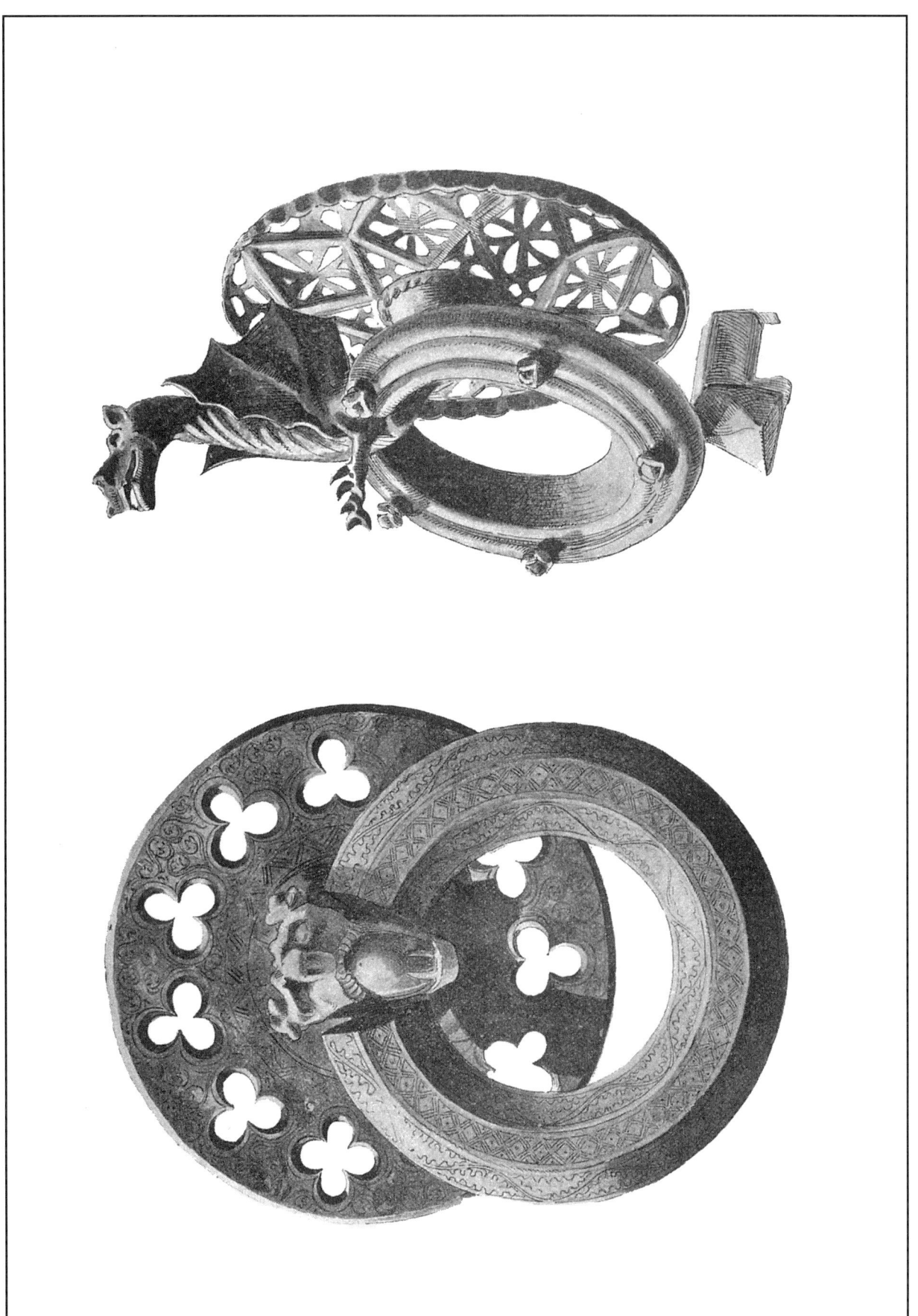

33. Door-knockers, French and Spanish (Catalan), 13th and 15th centuries

34. Door-knockers, Spanish (Castilian and Catalan), 16th century

35. Door-knockers, Spanish (Catalan), 15th and 16th centuries

36. Door-knockers, Spanish (Catalan), 15th and 16th centuries

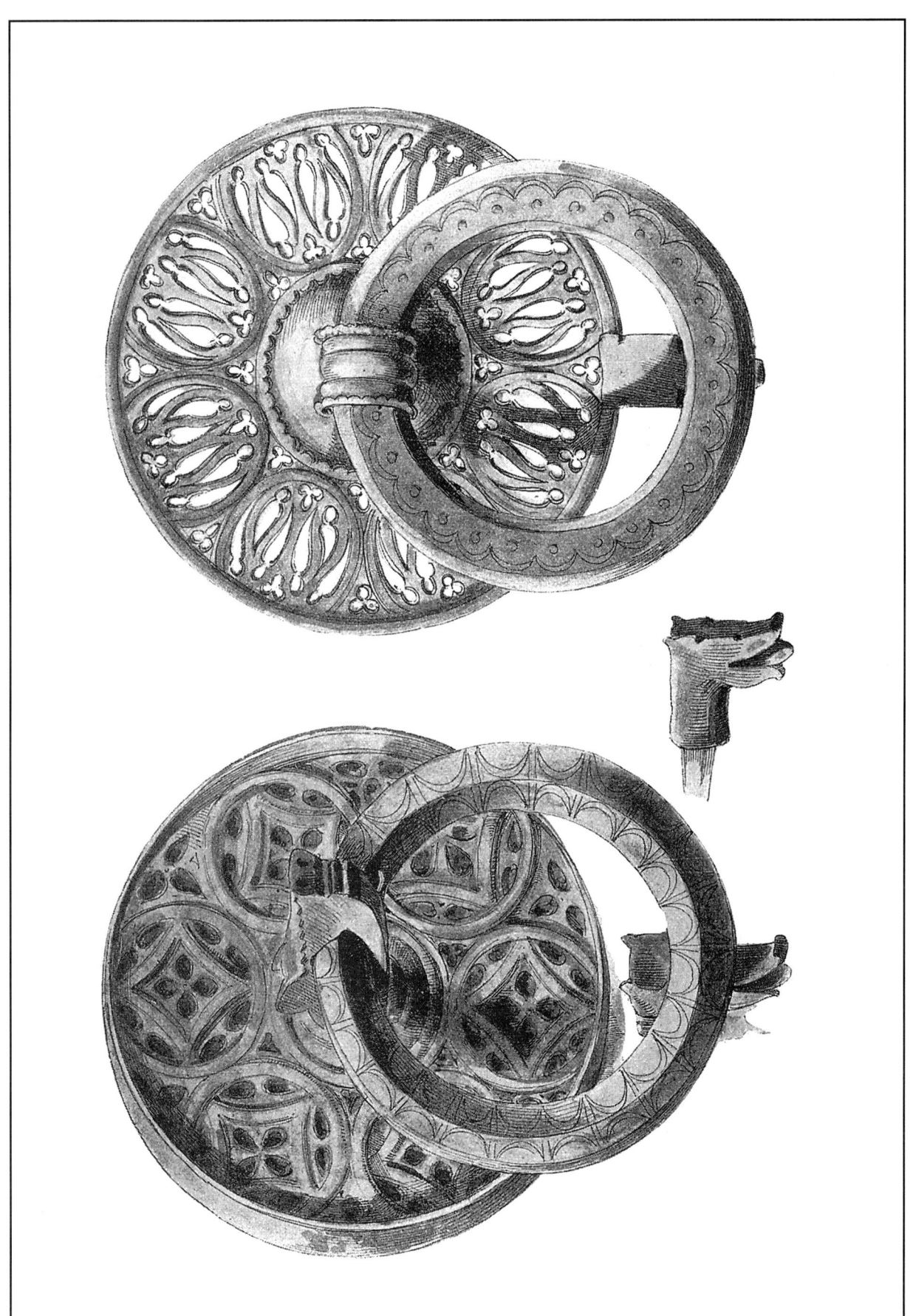

37. Door-knockers, Spanish (Catalan), 16th and 17th centuries

38. Door-knockers, Spanish (Catalan), 16th century

39. Door-knockers, Spanish (Catalan), 17th century

40. Abbey door, Spanish (Catalan), 10th, 11th and 12th centuries

41. Roman door, Spanish (Catalan), c. 10th–13th century

42. Small alcove door, Spanish (Catalan), 16th century

43. Embossed door studs, Spanish (Castilian), no date

44. Door, Spanish (Catalan), 12th century

45. Gridirons, Spanish, Flemish, and French, 17th century

46. Cathedral grille, Spanish (Castilian), 16th century

47. Cathedral grille, Spanish (Castilian), 16th century

48. Cathedral grille, Spanish (Castilian), 16th century

49. Cathedral grille, Spanish (Castilian), 16th century

50. Cathedral grille, Spanish (Castilian), 16th century

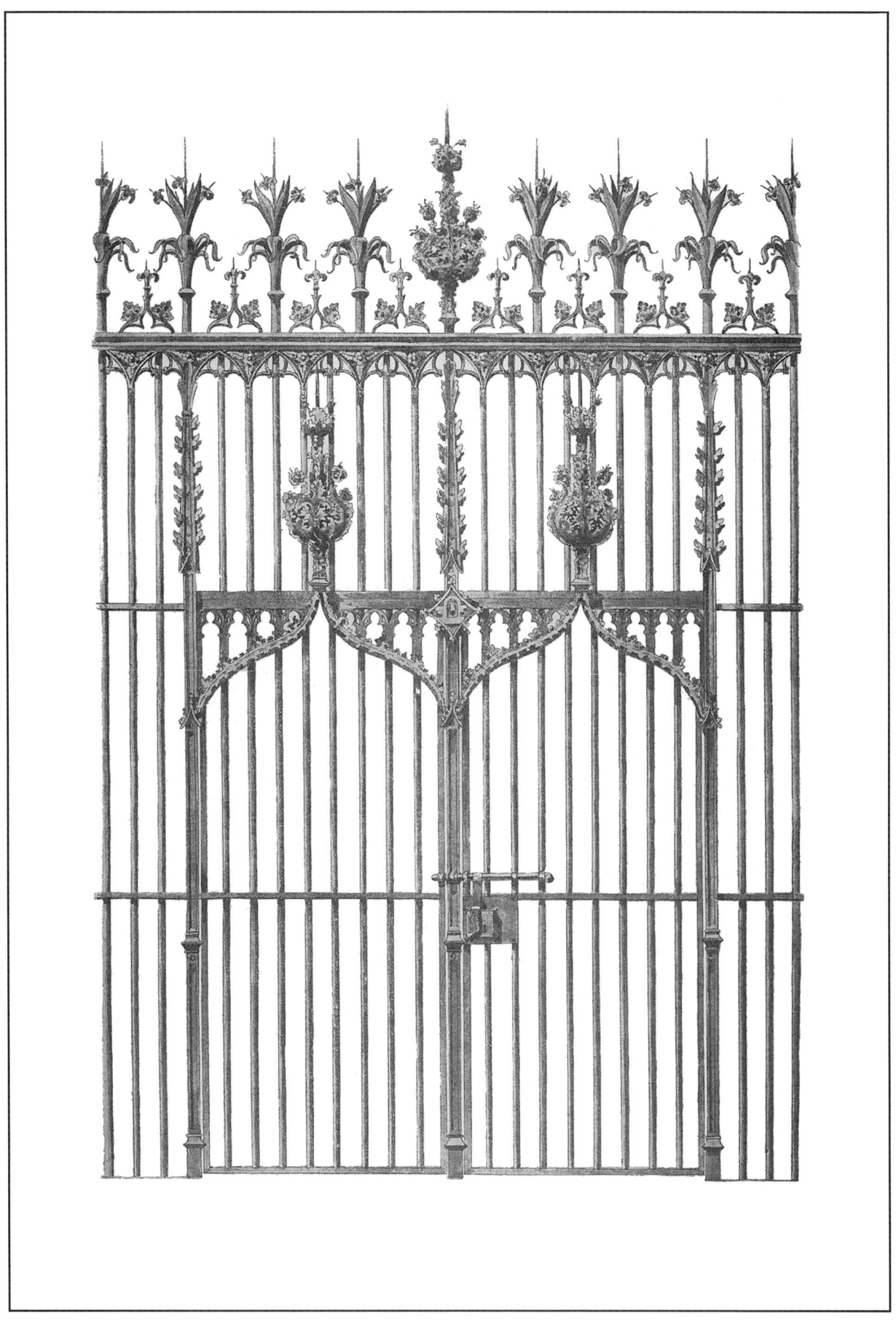

51. Cathedral grille, Spanish (Catalan), 15th and 16th centuries

52. Cathedral grille, Spanish (Catalan), 15th century

53. Cathedral grille, Spanish (Catalan), 15th century

54. Cathedral grille, Spanish (Catalan), 15th century

55. Cathedral grille, Spanish (Catalan), 16th century

56. Chapel grille, Spanish (Castilian), 16th century

57. Church grille, Spanish (Catalan), 16th century

58. Hospital pharmacy grille, Spanish (Catalan), 17th century

59. Palace door grille, Spanish, 18th century

60. Palace grille, Spanish (Castilian), 16th century

61. Palace grille, Spanish, 18th century

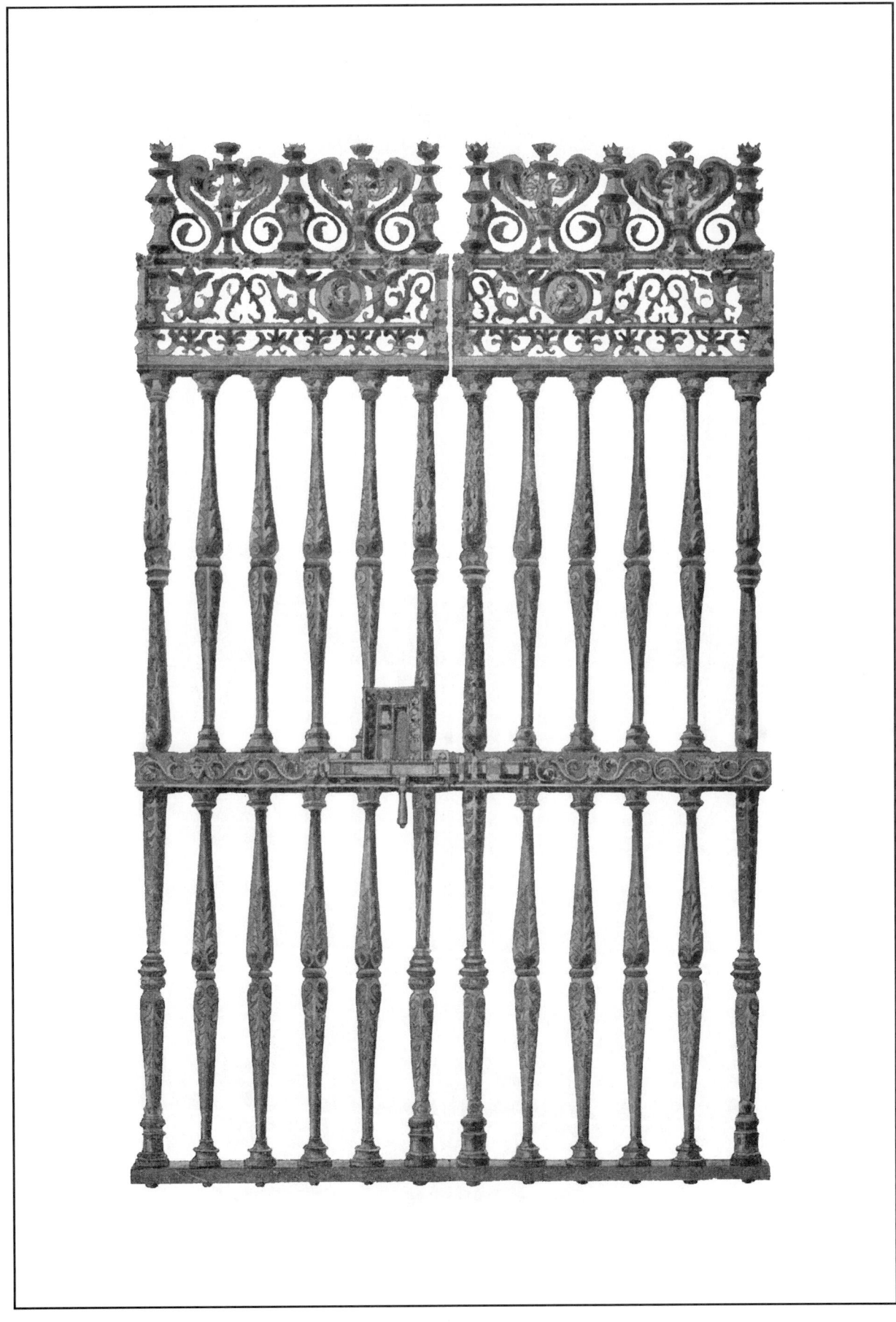

62. University library grille, Spanish (Castilian), 16th century

63. Grille and balcony railing, French and Spanish (Catalan), 16th and 18th centuries

64. Grille fragment, Spanish (Catalan), 11th or 12th century

65. Grille, Spanish (Castilian), 15th century

66. Grille, Spanish (Castilian), 16th century

67. Grille, Spanish (Castilian), 16th century

68. Grille, Spanish (Catalan), 13th, or beginning of 14th century

69. Grille, Spanish (Catalan), 15th century

70. Window grille, German and Spanish (Castilian), 15th and 16th centuries

71. Details of various grilles and embossed studs, Spanish (Catalan), 15th and 16th centuries

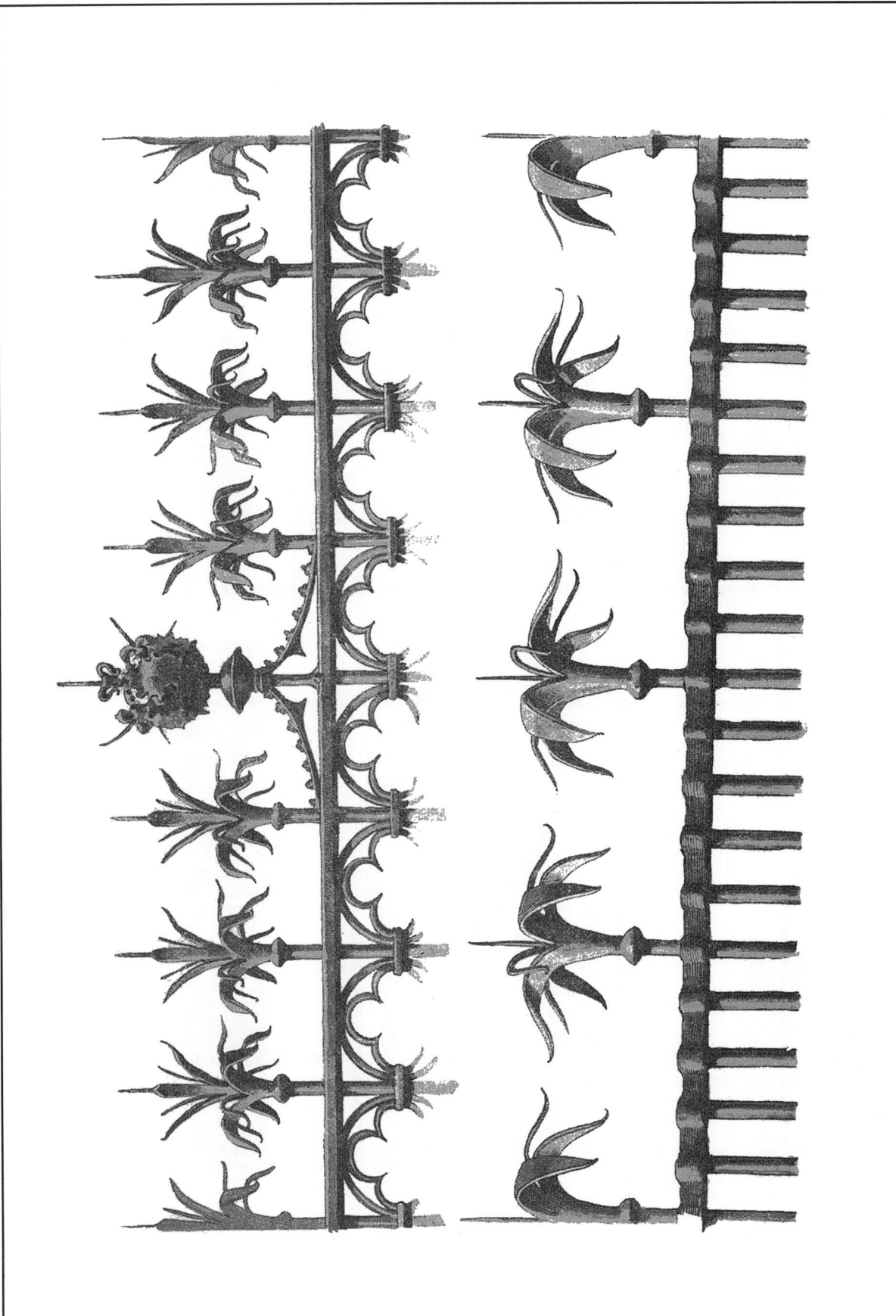

72. Top portions of two grilles, Spanish (Catalan), 16th century

73. Handles, pulls, and furniture hinges, German, French, and Spanish (Catalan), 15th century

74. Keys and locks, French and Spanish, 15th and 17th centuries

75. Keys, Spanish (Catalan), 14th, 15th, and 16th centuries

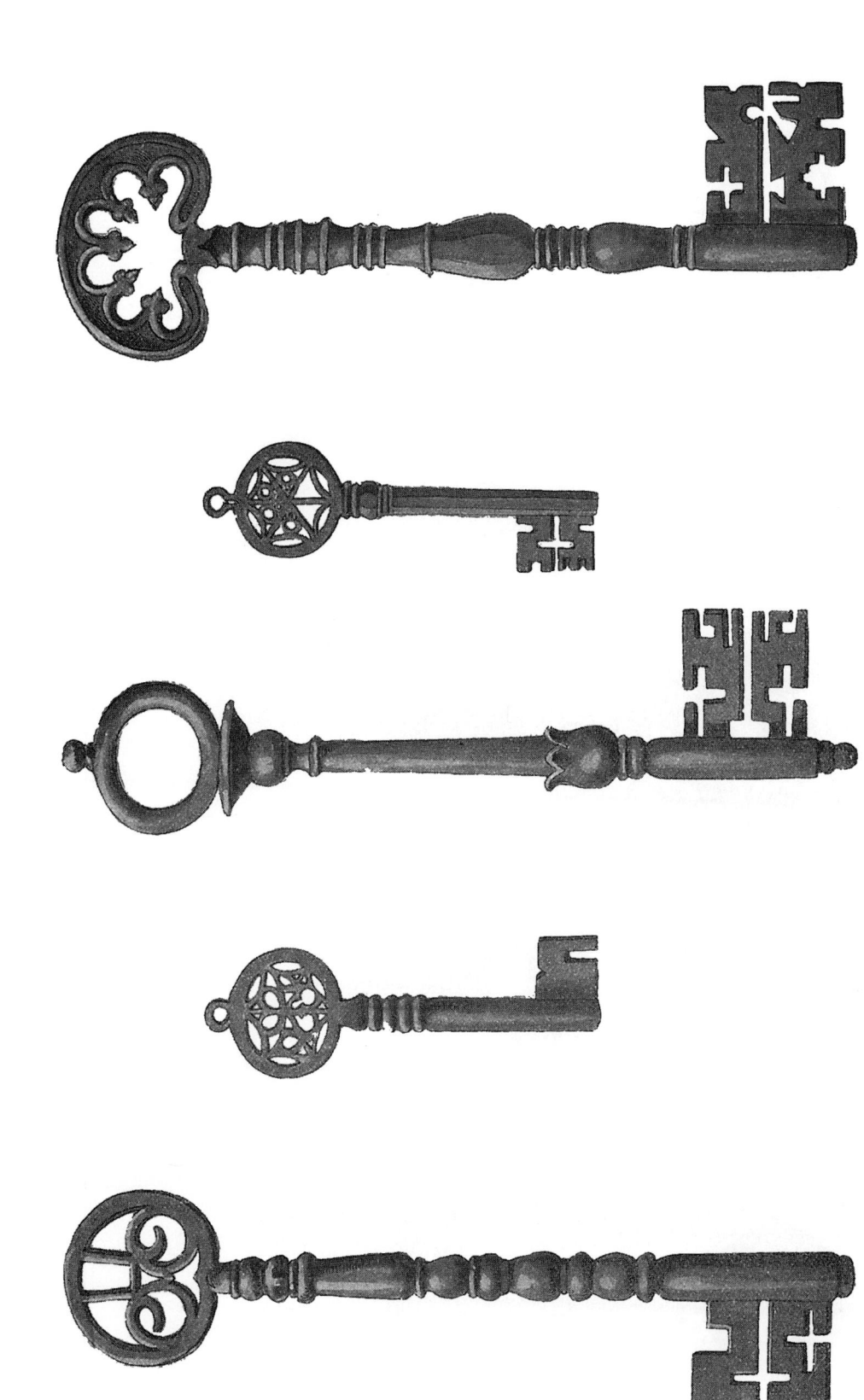

76. Keys, Spanish (Catalan), 17th century

77. Keys, Spanish (Catalan), 18th century

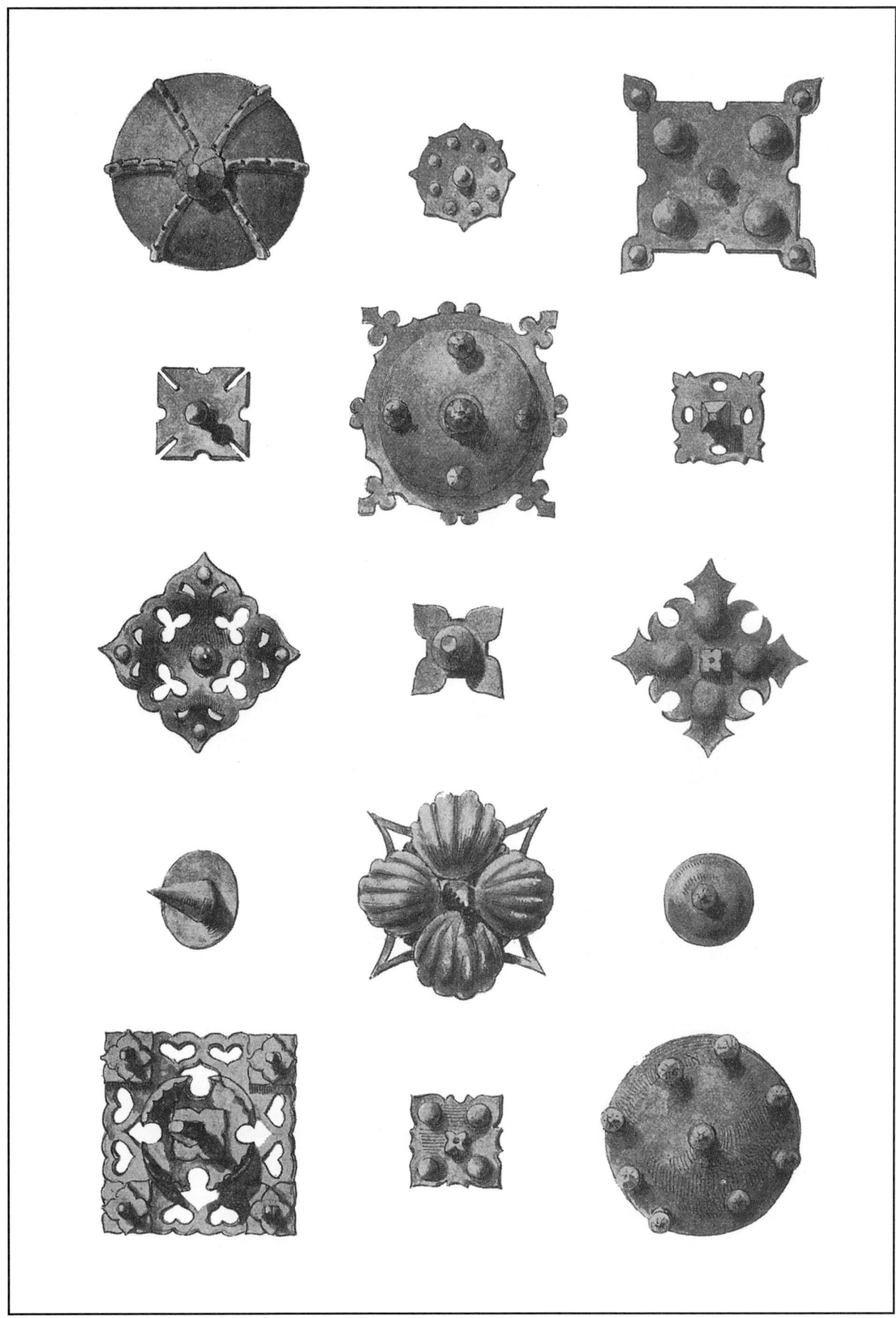

78. Embossed nailheads or studs, Spanish (Castilian), 15th, 16th, and 17th centuries

79. Pull-rings, door-knocker plate, and drawer-pull, German and Spanish, 15th and 16th centuries

80. Balcony railing, Spanish (Catalan), 18th century

81. Balcony railings, Spanish (Catalan), 18th century

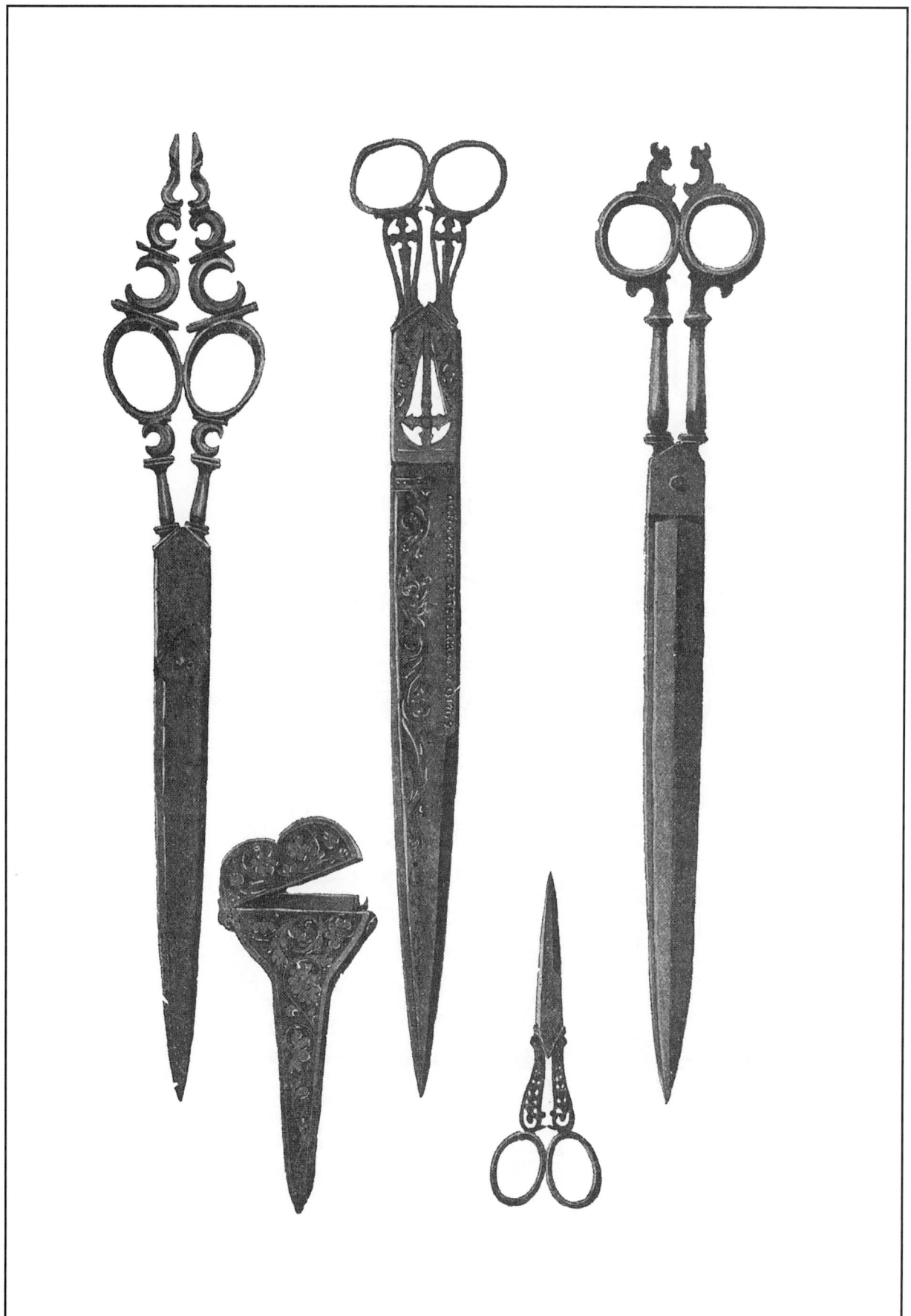

82. Scissors, Spanish, 17th and 18th centuries

83. Washstand and Weathervane, Italian and Spanish (Catalan), 15th century

84. Weathervane, Spanish (Catalan), 18th century

85. Framework of a well, Spanish (Catalan), 15th century

86. Andirons, French and Italian, 16th century

87. Andirons, French, 13th, 15th, and 16th centuries

88. Brackets and candelabra, French and Italian, 16th, 17th, and 18th centuries

89. Brackets and grille, French and German, 15th, 16th, and 18th centuries

90. Brackets, French, 18th century

91. Tripod brazier, tripod, Italian, 17th century

92. Chandelier, French or Italian, 15th century

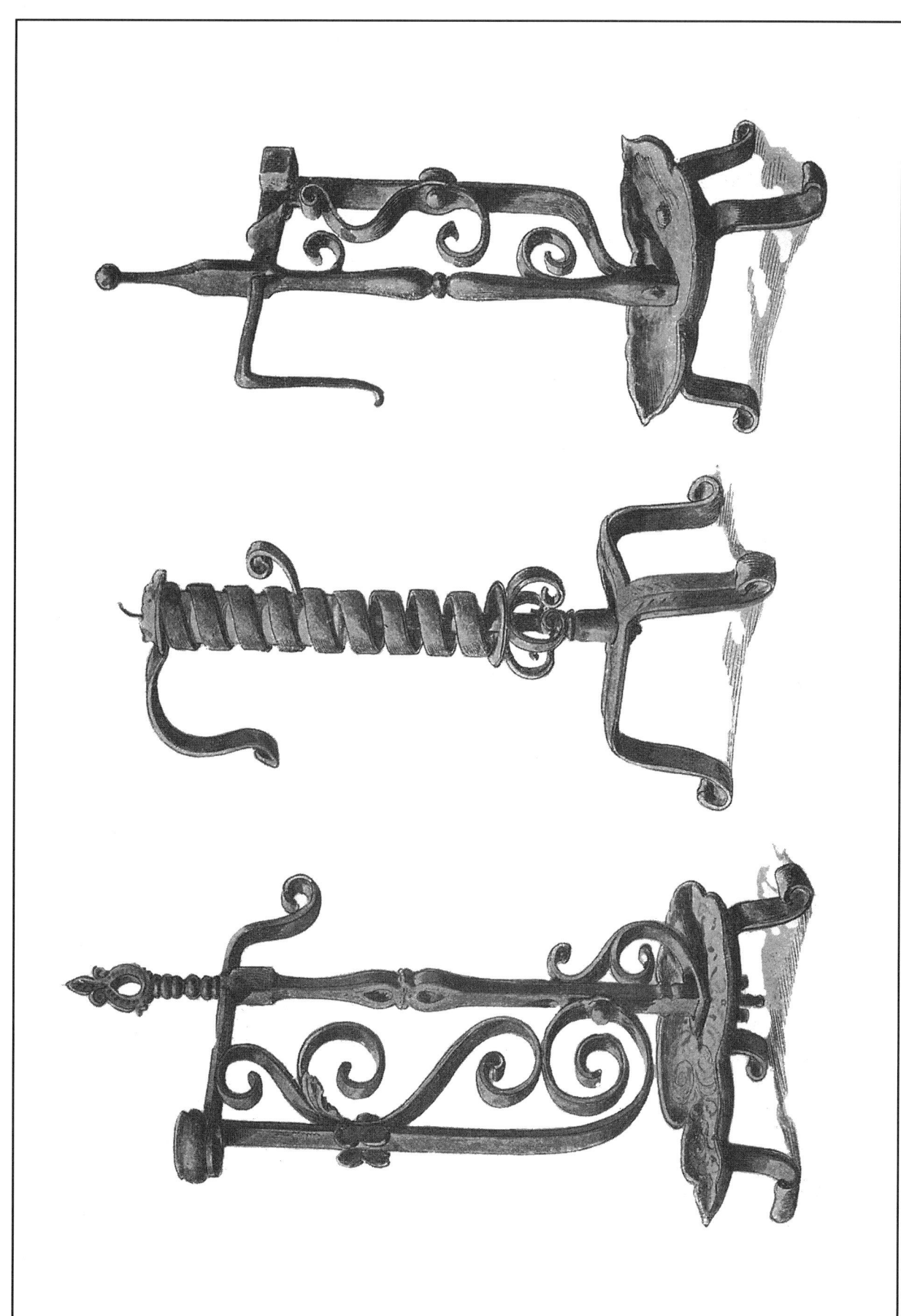

93. Chandeliers, French, 17th century

94. Door-handles, German, 15th century

95. Door-knocker plate and escutcheon (keyhole plate), German, 15th and 16th centuries

96. Door-knockers or pull-rings, German, 15th and 16th centuries

97. Door-knockers, Swiss and Italian, 15th and 17th centuries

98. Door hinges, French and German, 12th, 14th, and 17th centuries

99. Door, German, 15th century

100. Door, tabernacle, German, 14th century

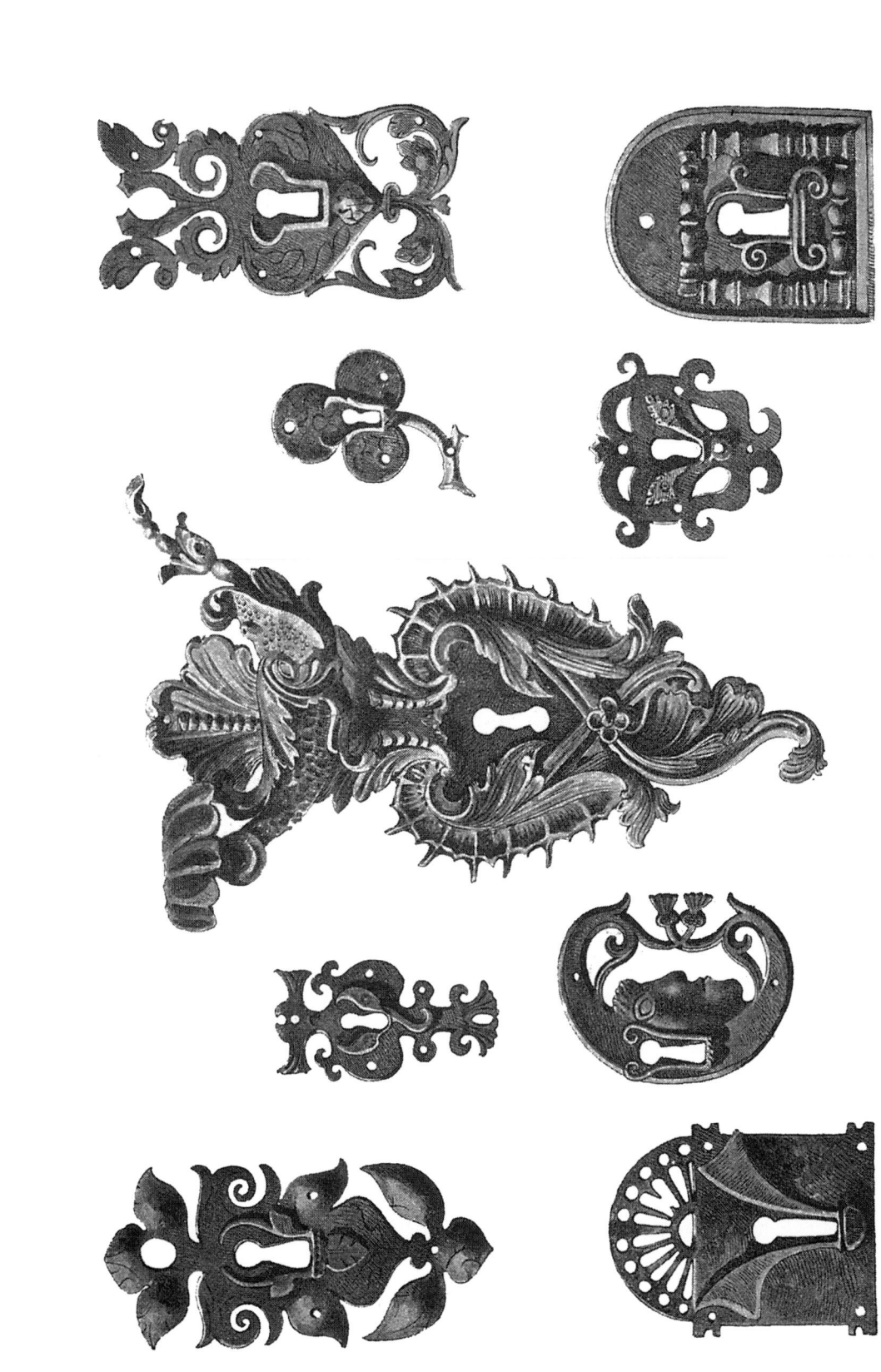

101. Escutcheons (keyhole plates), German, 16th, 17th, and 18th centuries

102. Chapel grille, Italian, 17th century

103. Door grille, French, 18th century

104. Church grille, French, 12th century

105. Section of a chapel grille, Italian, 16th century

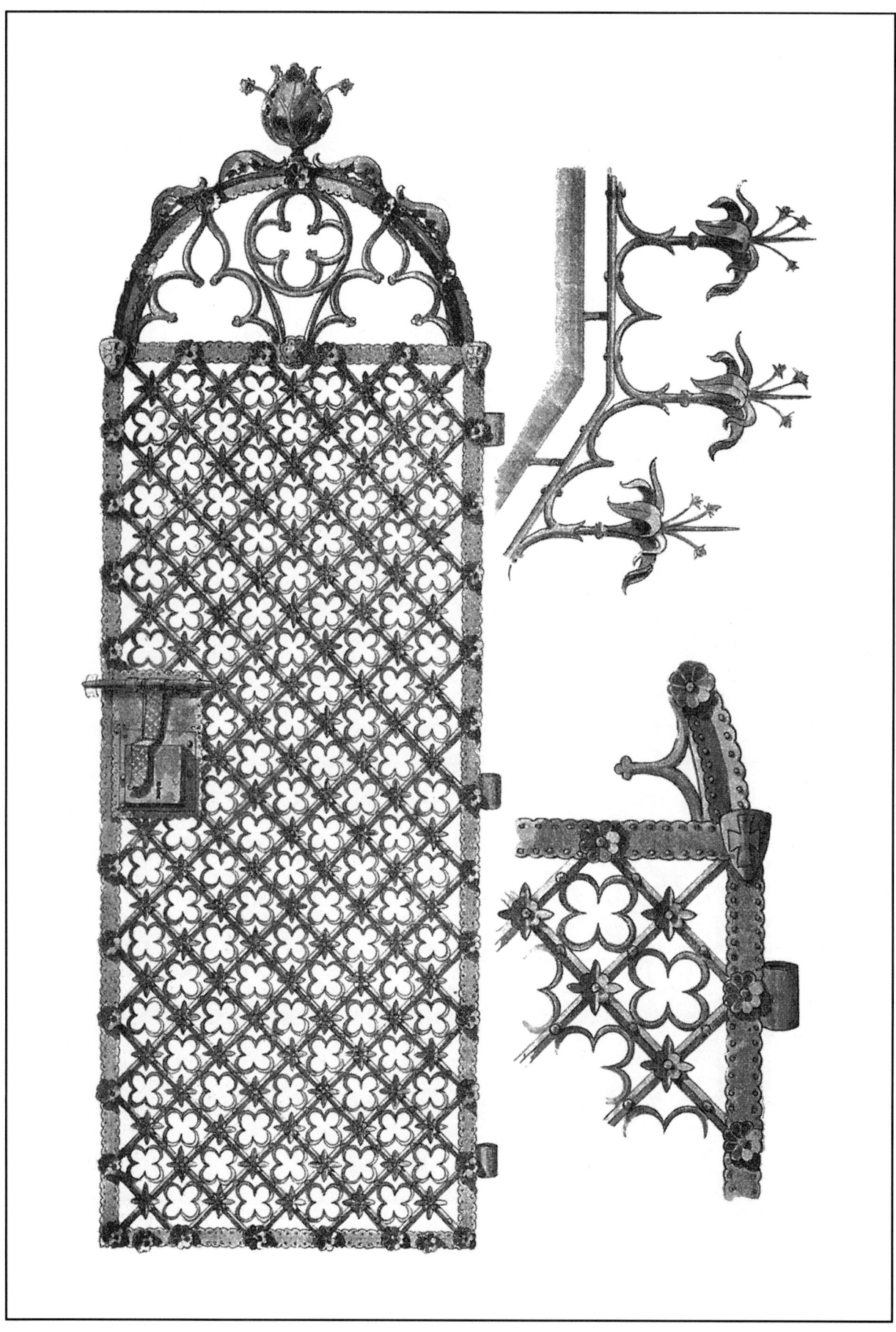

106. Cathedral grille, German, 15th century

107. Grille, French, 17th century

108. Grille, French, 17th century

109. Grille, French, 17th century

110. Grille, French, 18th century

111. Grille, French, 18th century

112. Grille, German, 15th century

113. Grille, German, 15th century

114. Grilles from a carriage entrance, German, 16th century

115. Furniture hinges, escutcheons (keyhole plates), and embossed stud, German, 15th century

116. Keys and locks, French and German, 15th and 17th centuries

117. Lock, key, and furniture bolt, French, 13th and 14th centuries

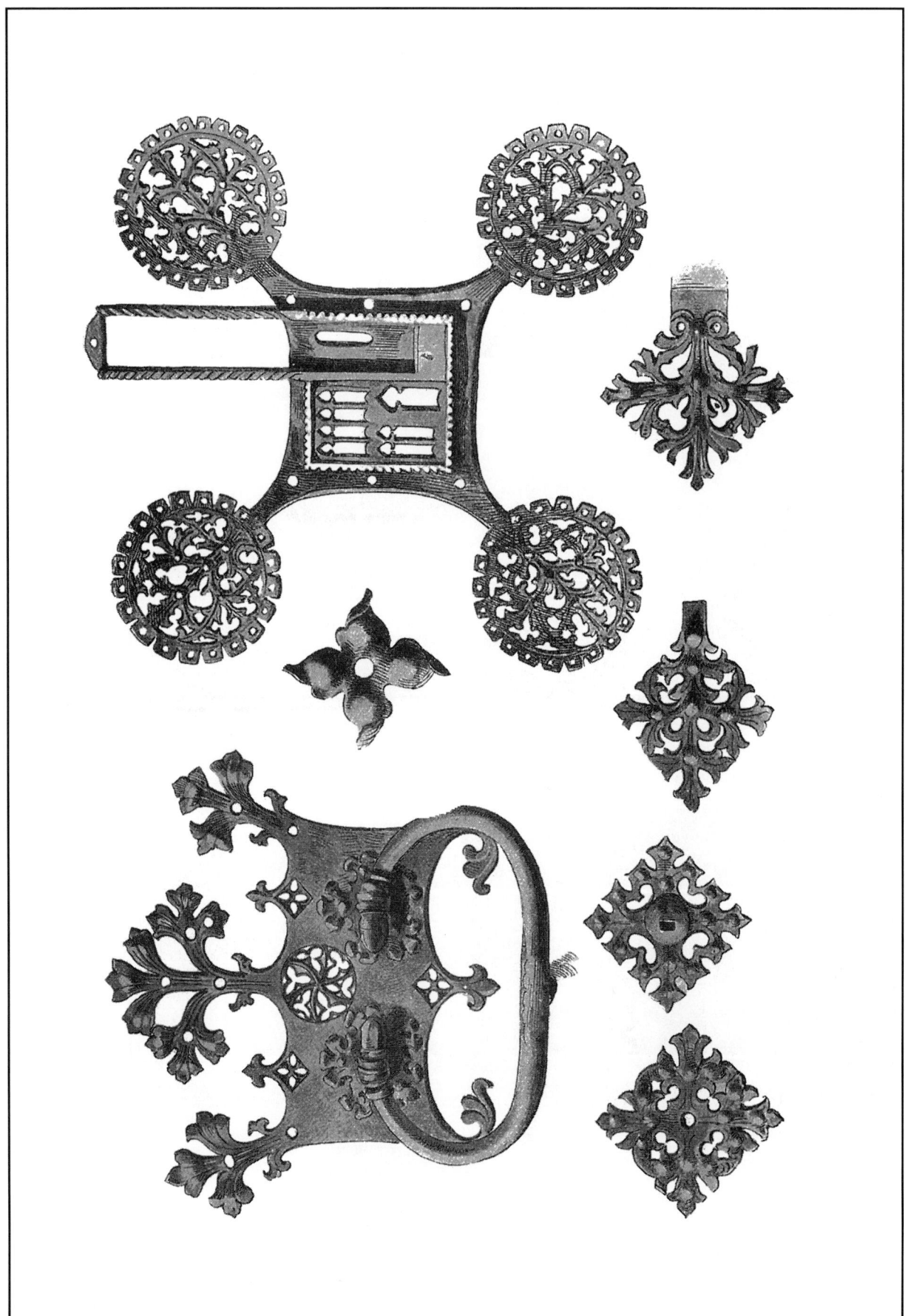

118. Pull-ring, lock, and embossed corner studs, German, 15th century

119. Staircase and balcony railings, French, 18th century

120. Sign or emblem bracket and hinge, German, 15th and 16th centuries